Scrambled Bugs

Don't let this page bug you! Just unscramble these insect names, then put the numbered letters in the correct spaces below to reveal the answer to the riddle.

TAN (A)(N)(T)
2

THOM ◯◯◯◯
4

LEAF ◯◯◯◯
7

PAWS ◯◯◯◯
6

KICT ◯◯◯◯
3

TANG ◯◯◯◯
11

LEETEB ◯◯◯◯◯◯
12

DEBUBG ◯◯◯◯◯◯
8

KITCREC ◯◯◯◯◯◯◯
10

SOOQTUIM ◯◯◯◯◯◯◯◯
5

GANDRYFLO ◯◯◯◯◯◯◯◯◯
1

GRAPHPOSERS ◯◯◯◯◯◯◯◯◯◯◯
9

Where does a spider keep its photos?

◯(N) ◯◯◯ ◯◯◯◯◯ ◯◯◯
1 2   3 4 5   6 7 8 9 10   11 12

ANT
MOTH
FLEA
WASP
TICK
GNAT
BEETLE
BEDBUG
CRICKET
MOSQUITO
DRAGONFLY
GRASSHOPPER

Where does a spider
keep its photos?
ON ITS WEBSITE

Morning Yoga

What things in this picture are silly? It's up to you!

Why does a flamingo stand on one leg?

If it lifted both legs, it would fall over!

What band plays music that makes you want to stretch?

A rubber band

Knock, knock.

Who's there?

Mice.

Mice who?

Mice to see you at yoga today!

What is an elephant's favorite sport?

Squash

Art by David Coulson

K-9 Academy

Can you help these pups figure out the punch lines?
To solve these riddles, use the fractions of the words given below.

Why was the dog excited to go to school?

Last ⅓ of BUS
First ½ of MEOW
Last ½ of PULL
Last ⅗ of SWING
First ¼ of BALL
Last ½ of TREE

The class was having a

☐☐☐☐☐☐☐☐

☐☐☐.

Why did the dog study before class?

First ⅓ of PURPLE
Last ¼ of JUMP
First ⅖ of QUEEN
Last ⅓ of SKI
First ⅕ of ZEBRA

In case the teacher gave a

☐☐☐ ☐☐☐☐

BONUS: How many bones can you find in this scene?

Why was the dog
excited to go to school?
**The class was having a
SMELLING BEE.**

Why did the dog study
before class?
**In case the teacher gave
a PUP QUIZ**

BONUS:
There are **40** bones.

Best _____ Ever!
NOUN

This is best played with a friend or family member. Without letting them read the story, ask for the words or phrases under the blanks. (For example, the first thing you'll ask for is a big number.) When all the blanks are filled, read the story out loud.

Last night, I had the *best* sleepover for my birthday. _____ friends came
BIG NUMBER

over. We went down to the basement, where I saw a(n) _____ _____
COLOR   JUNGLE ANIMAL

hanging birthday decorations. _____ was hungry and ate _____
FRIEND'S NAME   YUCKY FOOD

dipped in cold, creamy _____. Then we watched the same episode of
PLURAL NOUN

_____ _____ times. My little brother kept _____, but my friends
TV SHOW   BIG NUMBER   -ING VERB

said their _____ did the same thing at their houses.
PLURAL NOUN

For dinner, we had deep-fried, _____-flavored hot dogs and an
FLAVOR OF ICE CREAM

extra-large bowl of_____. Yum! For dessert, we ate a(n) _____
FOOD YOU DON'T LIKE   COLOR

_____ cake. Everyone sang _____.
VEGETABLE   YOUR FAVORITE SONG

Later, _____ came over for a huge pillow fight. It was so _____!
FAMOUS PERSON   ADJECTIVE

Mom told us to clean up, and I vacuumed up the _____ hy mistake.
BIG PIECE OF FURNITURE

It was a(n) _____ party. The only sad part was that _____ felt
ADJECTIVE   SAME FRIEND'S NAME

sick in the middle of the _____ and went home riding a(n) _____.
NOUN   INSECT

Art by Sara Varon

Are You Kitten Me?

Each cat has one that matches it exactly.
Pair up the cats to match each riddle with its punch line.

____ **1.** What happened when the cat ate a ball of yarn?

A. *Purr*-ple

 ____ **2.** What do you call a cat drinking lemonade?

B. "Me-OUCH!"

____ **3.** What did the cat say when he stubbed his toe?

C. A sourpuss

 ____ **4.** What is a cat's favorite color?

D. Alley cats

____ **5.** What cats like to go bowling?

E. She had mittens.

Art by Carolina Farias

Just Sayin'

Give this bird something to say. Then find the hidden
CHAIR, **FISH**, **MARKER**, **SLICE OF PIZZA**, and **STOPWATCH**.

Art by James Kochalka

Pie Path

Peri just pulled her pie from the oven. Can you help her get it to the pie-baking contest before it cools? When you're done, write the letters along the way in the spaces below to answer the riddle.

What is the best thing to put in a pie?

_ _ _ _ _   _ _ _ _ _

START

FINISH

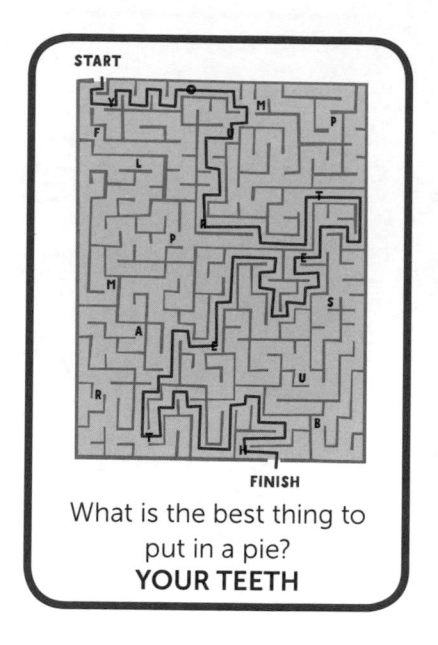

START

FINISH

What is the best thing to
put in a pie?
YOUR TEETH

Turtle Crossing

To get the answer to the riddle below, first cross out all the pairs of matching letters. Then write the remaining letters in order in the spaces below the riddle.

QQ	EE	BB	ON	MM	OO	WW
LL	PP	SS	VV	YY	ZZ	EM
II	AA	RR	NN	EE	IL	YY
HH	XX	PP	DD	EP	UU	SS
GG	OO	ER	SS	CC	QQ	II
CC	YY	EE	MM	AA	TT	HO
UU	BB	KK	VV	ZZ	UR	TT

What was the turtle doing on the highway?

___ ___ ___   ___ ___ ___ ___

___ ___ ___

___ ___ ___ ___

SLOW

Art by Brian Whitea

What was the turtle
doing on the highway?
ONE MILE PER HOUR

Duck Drop

Only six of the letters in the top line will work their way through this maze to land in the numbered spaces at the bottom. When they get there, they will spell out the answer to the riddle.

D I B U L X E R E D O O E

1 2 3 4 5 6

What does a duck wear when he gets married?

A _ _ _ _ _ _
  1 2 3 4 5 6

Art by Brian White

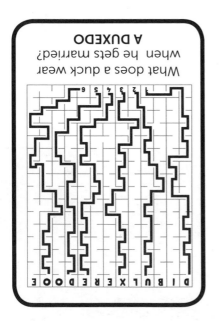

A DUXEDO

What does a duck wear
when he gets married?

Hidden Words

There are five words (not pictures!) hidden in the scene below. Can you find them all? Once you do, arrange the words in order to give this joke a punch line!

Knock, knock.
Who's there?
Canoe.
Canoe who?

__ __ __ __ __ __   __ __ __ __ __

__ __ __   __ __ __   __ __ __ __?

Art by Kelly Kennedy

Knock, knock.
Who's there?
Canoe.
Canoe who?
CANOE COME OUT AND PLAY?

Grocery Giggles

What things in this picture are silly? It's up to you!

PRODUCE

BUY EGGS!

3⁹⁴   1⁷⁹

TODAY'S SPECIAL

LAST WEEK'S SPECIAL

ASSORTED FLOWERS $9⁹⁹

What do you get if you drop a basket of fruit?

Fruit salad

Where do sheep keep their groceries?

In their grocery baa-skets

Why did the vegetable band break up?

It didn't have a beet.

What did the snowman buy at the grocery store?

Icebergers

Art by Pat Lewis

Roundabout

To solve this riddle, start at the arrow. Then count around the wheel to every third letter, writing those letters in order in the space below. Keep going until you've been to each letter exactly once.

START

Why did the chicken cross the water park?

T O _ _ _ _ _ _ _ _

_ _ _ _ _ _ _ _

_ _ _ _ _

Art by Carolina Farias

Why did the chicken
cross the water park?
**TO GET TO THE
OTHER SLIDE**

A Teacher's _____
NOUN

This is best played with a friend or family member. Without letting them read the story, ask for the words or phrases under the blanks. (For example, the first thing you'll ask for is a friend's first name.) When all the blanks are filled, read the story out loud.

Dear Parent,

_____ has been an absolute _____
FRIEND'S FIRST NAME   NOUN

to teach this year. Never before have I seen a student

quite so _____ and _____, truly the
ADJECTIVE   ADJECTIVE

class _____! On the first day of school,
NOUN

_____ explained The Theory of _____ to
SAME FIRST NAME   VEGETABLE (PLURAL)

the whole class. One day in art class, your child did a sculpture of

a(n) _____ and it sold for _____ dollars to a
SCARY INSECT   HIGH NUMBER

collector on _____.
PLANET OTHER THAN EARTH

However, not everything has been _____. Your child
ADJECTIVE

likes to _____ class discussion. It's not fair—there are
VERB

other _____ in the room! And in gym class, it
PLURAL NOUN

would be nice if your child wouldn't _____ all over
VERB

the basketball court. As for hygiene, this student doesn't seem to

understand basic concepts such as _____ or how to
-ING VERB

_____ a _____. All in all, your child is a real
VERB   NOUN

_____ of a student, and I am soooo glad I've decided to
TYPE OF FRUIT

leave teaching for good.

Sincerely,
Mrs. Woodard

Art by Kelly Kennedy

Books Never Written

Can you match each of these 10 funny book titles to their author?
Try reading the author names out loud!

____ **1.** *Anatomy of a Shark*

____ **2.** *Face to Face with a Bear*

____ **3.** *How to Catch Worms*

____ **4.** *Big Green Snakes*

____ **5.** *The World of Apes*

____ **6.** *Where Are All the Lemurs?*

____ **7.** *Itchy Bugs*

____ **8.** *Where's My Tuxedo?*

____ **9.** *What Dogs Do*

____ **10.** *Before the Cocoon*

A. Amos Keeto

B. Heidi Bones

C. Jim Panzee

D. Kat R. Pillar

E. Penny Gwinn

F. Rosa Teeth

G. Terry Fied

H. Earl E. Bird

I. Maddie Gascar

J. Anna Conda

HOW BIG Are Hippos? BY Hugh Mongus

Freeway Free-for-All

Can you help Carl navigate the freeway to get home in time for dinner? When you're done, write the letters along the way in the spaces below to answer the riddle.

FINISH

START

What driver never drives a car?

__ _____

Art by Mike Moran

What driver never
drives a car?
A SCREWDRIVER

Quacker Code

It's your ducky day! Each funny duck below represents a letter.
Use the code to solve the ducky riddles.

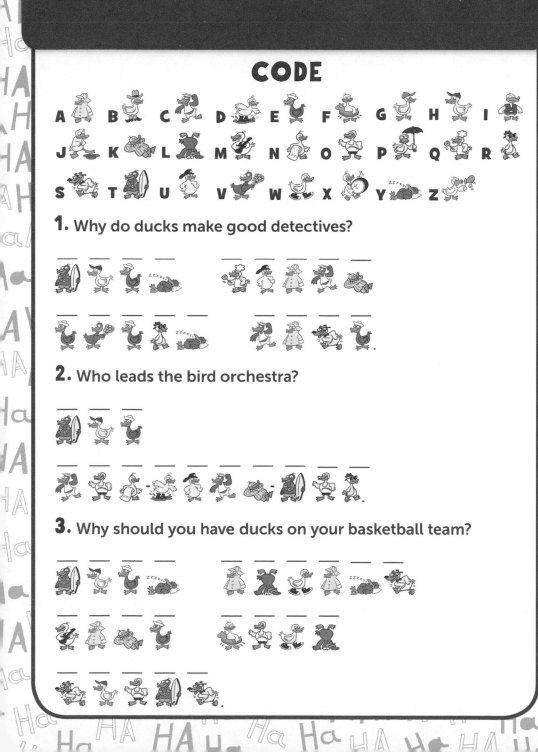

CODE

1. Why do ducks make good detectives?

2. Who leads the bird orchestra?

3. Why should you have ducks on your basketball team?

Art by Kelly Kennedy

Why do ducks make good detectives?
THEY QUACK EVERY CASE.

Who leads the bird orchestra?
THE CON-DUCK-TOR

Why should you have ducks on your basketball team?
THEY ALWAYS MAKE FOWL SHOTS.

Sun Drop

To read the joke and punch line, move the letters from each column into the boxes directly above them to form words. But watch out: the letters do not always go in the boxes in the same order as they appear. Each letter is only used once.

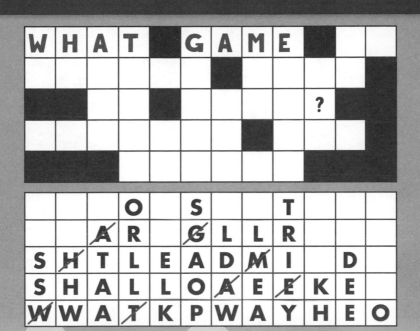

| W | H | A | T | | G | A | M | E | | |

| | | | | | | | | | | ? |

O		S			T	
A̶	R	G̶	L	L	R	
S̶	H	T	L	E	A	D	M̶	I	D
S	H	A	L	L	O	A̶	E̶	E̶	K	E
W	W	A	T̶	K	P	W	A	Y	H	E	O

Art by Rich Powell

WHAT GAME DO
SHARKS LIKE TO PLAY?
SWALLOW THE LEADER

The Comedy Coop

These chickens are cracking up! To join the fun, read each riddle, then unscramble the letters on the eggs for the answers.

Art by Pat Lewis

Which birds are sad?
BLUE JAYS

What can turkeys use to
play an instrument?
DRUMSTICKS

What do you give a
sick bird?
TWEET-MENT

What are smarter than
talking birds?
SPELLING BEES

What do you get when
you cross centipedes
with parrots?
WALKIE-TALKIES

That's Just Ducky!

What things in this picture are silly? It's up to you!

What time do ducks wake up?
At the quack of dawn

If you try to cross a lake in a leaky boat, what do you get?
About halfway

Knock, knock.
Who's there?
Water.
Water who?
Water you waiting for? Let me in!

How do you catch a rare animal?
Unique up on it.

Art by Dave Klug

Math Mirth

The Math Club is having its annual comedy night.
To solve these riddles, use the fractions of the words given below.

Why did the math teacher stop singing karaoke?

____ _____ ____ ____.

Last ³⁄₅ of **USHER**
Middle ⅓ of **MANUAL**
Last ½ of **CUCUMBER**
Middle ⅓ of **BEWARE**
First ⅓ of **SUPERSTAR**

What do math teachers eat?

_ _ _ _ _ _
_ _ _ _ _

First ½ of **SQUASH**
First ⅓ of **ARTIST**
Last ½ of **POEM**
Last ½ of **CONCEALS**

Art by Mike Moran

Why did the math teacher stop singing karaoke?

HER NUMBER WAS UP.

What do math teachers eat?

SQUARE MEALS

A New School _____!
NOUN

This is best played with a friend or family member. Without letting them read the story, ask for the words or phrases under the blanks. (For example, the first thing you'll ask for is a friend's first name.) When all the blanks are filled, read the story out loud.

"Welcome, students of the _____ Q. _____ School,
FRIEND'S FIRST NAME   VEGETABLE

this is your new principal. This school year is going to be _____. First
ADJECTIVE

of all, our school has been relocated to Western _____,
PLANET OTHER THAN EARTH

and you'll be attending only two days a week! Plus, all teachers must dye their hair

_____ with _____ polka dots and stars. But it won't be all fun
COLOR   ANOTHER COLOR

and _____, I promise you. The cafeteria will only serve deep-fried
PLURAL NOUN

_____, and the hall monitor will be a(n) _____. There
FOOD YOU DON'T LIKE   KIND OF FISH

will be _____ million hours of homework every night, and all students
VERY HIGH NUMBER

must be accompanied to and from school by a floating _____. If not,
HOUSEHOLD APPLIANCE

I will personally call your _____. On the other hand, students automatically get
NOUN

every test answer right and a locker full of _____, too. Today's news may
PLURAL NOUN

seem strange to you, but I've been principal for about _____ minutes now,
LOW NUMBER

and I know exactly what I'm doing!"

Unidentified UFOs!

UFO usually stands for Unidentified Flying Object.
Can you use the clues to identify the rest of these UFOs?

1. Large, sad, flightless bird in Paris

2. Lint-covered breakfast food

3. Wise winged girls in the city

4. Unattractive hopping robber

5. Root vegetable from Tallahassee

6. Hilarious policeman

7. Icy and pristine Atlantic

A. Ugly Frog Outlaw

B. Undisturbed Frozen Ocean

C. Upper Florida Onion

D. Unhappy French Ostrich

E. Unbelievably Funny Officer

F. Urban Female Owls

G. Untouched Fuzzy Oatmeal

Art by Jim Paillot

Just Sayin'

Give this boy something to say. Then find the hidden
CAT, **CARROT**, **ENVELOPE**, **ICE-CREAM CONE**, and **LADDER**.

Art by James Kochalka

Pond Hopping

It's a funny day at Froggy Pond! To spell out the answer to this riddle, find the correct path from frog to log.

O N J U S
M S Z F H D R
T E B A C A
A N S I L P
O L L Y G
I N X Q K P

FINISH

START

Where do funny frogs sit?

__ __   __ __ __ __   __ __ __

Art by Constanza Basaluzzo

ON SILLY PADS
Where do funny frogs sit?

Cow Chuckles

To figure out this riddle, follow the directions below. Each sentence will tell you where one letter is in the grid. Once you've found it, write it in the correct space below the riddle.

1. This letter appears side by side in the same row.

2. This letter is the only vowel in the first row.

3. This letter is two down from the **B**.

4. This letter is the first and last in its row.

5. This is the second-to-last letter in the third row.

6. Look two above the **Y** for this letter.

7. This letter is sandwiched between two **M**'s.

8. This letter is the last letter in the grid.

What does a cow use to cut grass?

$\overline{\quad}\;\; \overline{\quad}\;\overline{\quad}\;\overline{\quad}\;\overline{\quad}\text{-}\overline{\quad}\;\overline{\quad}\;\overline{\quad}\text{-}\overline{\quad}$
 4   8   4   3   1   5   6   6   2   7

M	B	X	H	Q	E	Z
S	Z	O	P	F	T	G
A	W	E	D	J	M	A
L	U	Y	M	R	M	K
Q	J	F	O	N	N	S
C	R	D	V	X	G	L

What does a cow
use to cut grass?
A LAWN-*MOO*-ER

All Knight Drop

To read the joke and punch line, move the letters from each column into the boxes directly above them to form words. But watch out: the letters do not always go in the boxes in the same order as they appear. Each letter is only used once.

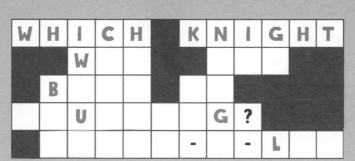

W	H	I	C	H	■	K	N	I	G	H	T
■	■	W			■					■	■
■	B				■			■	■	■	■
		U					G	?	■	■	■
■						-		-	L		

		A	S	~~H~~			T				
	~~B~~	~~I~~	A	T			~~G~~				
	~~H~~	~~W~~	~~C~~	C		N	A		~~L~~		
~~W~~	L	~~U~~	N	T	E	~~K~~	T	H	~~G~~	O	T
J	O	E	S	S	I	A	~~N~~	~~I~~	E	~~H~~	~~T~~

TODAY'S LESSON
WINGS
SPIKES
POINTY TEETH
FIRE BREATH
LONG TAIL
THE KINGDOM

Art by Jef Czekaj

Mixed Breeds

We've jumbled the names of 10 dog breeds. Can you unscramble each set of letters and find all the breeds? Once you have them all, read down the column of boxes to learn the answer to the riddle.

What do you call a dog who helps you carry hot things?

GLEABE   _ _ ▢ _ _ _

TAGRE NEAD   _ _ _ _ _ _ _ _ ▢ _

ICELLO   _ ▢ _ _ _ _

TREERIVER   _ _ _ _ _ _ _ ▢ _ _

EXBRO   _ _ _ ▢ _

EALSPIN   _ _ _ ▢ _ _ _

BARNDOME   _ _ ▢ _ _ _ _ _

SKYUH   _ ▢ _ _ _

TIP LUBL   _ _ ▢ _ _ _ _ _

SHIRI STREET   _ _ _ _ _ _ ▢ _ _ _ _ _

Art by Kelly Kennedy

BEAGLE   SPANIEL
GREAT   DOBERMAN
  DANE   HUSKY
COLLIE   PIT BULL
RETRIEVER   IRISH
BOXER   SETTER

What do you call a dog who
helps you carry hot things?
AN OVEN MUTT

Bowling Bonanza

What things in this picture are silly? It's up to you!

What are old bowling balls used for?

Marbles for elephants

What makes a bowler happy and a batter sad?

"Strike!"

What happens when a pig loses a bowling match?

He becomes disgruntled.

Knock, knock.
Who's there?
Annie.
Annie who?
Annie body want to bowl?

Robot Ramble

Cross out all the boxes in which the number can be evenly divided by 3.
Then write the leftover letters in the spaces to spell the answer.

33 H	31 T	9 R	17 O	13 R	42 Q	8 E	27 Z	10 C	39 A	91 H
24 B	54 Y	37 A	55 R	12 L	2 G	60 W	11 E	18 M	23 H	77 I
30 F	43 S	36 N	22 B	35 A	90 E	3 O	38 T	21 K	5 T	99 S
81 D	18 V	43 E	45 C	53 R	15 J	28 I	46 E	54 P	6 B	19 S

Why did the robot go on vacation?

__ __   __ __ __ __ __ __ __ __

__ __ __ __ __ __ __ __ __ __ __

Why did the robot
go on vacation?
**TO RECHARGE
HIS BATTERIES**

Ready for a Pet _____
ANIMAL

This is best played with a friend or family member. Without letting them read the story, ask for the words or phrases under the blanks. (For example, the first thing you'll ask for is your city or town.) When all the blanks are filled, read the story out loud.

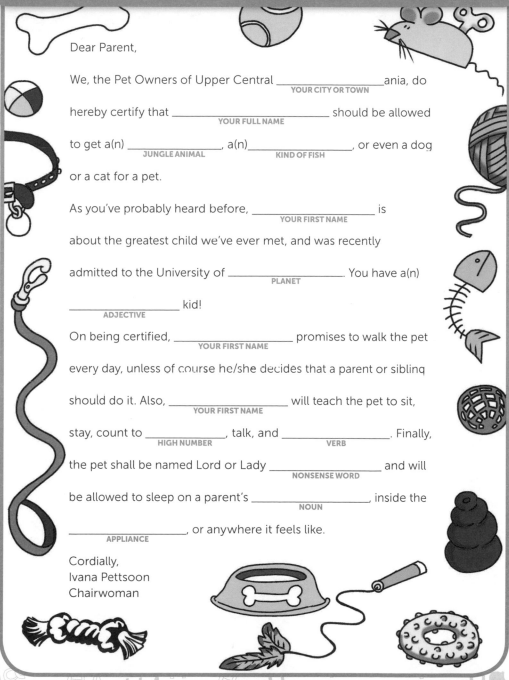

Dear Parent,

We, the Pet Owners of Upper Central _____ania, do
                                    YOUR CITY OR TOWN

hereby certify that _____ should be allowed
                              YOUR FULL NAME

to get a(n) _____, a(n)_____, or even a dog
              JUNGLE ANIMAL   KIND OF FISH

or a cat for a pet.

As you've probably heard before, _____ is
                                    YOUR FIRST NAME

about the greatest child we've ever met, and was recently

admitted to the University of _____. You have a(n)
                                    PLANET

_____ kid!
      ADJECTIVE

On being certified, _____ promises to walk the pet
                        YOUR FIRST NAME

every day, unless of course he/she decides that a parent or sibling

should do it. Also, _____ will teach the pet to sit,
                        YOUR FIRST NAME

stay, count to _____, talk, and _____. Finally,
                  HIGH NUMBER   VERB

the pet shall be named Lord or Lady _____ and will
                                          NONSENSE WORD

be allowed to sleep on a parent's _____, inside the
                                        NOUN

_____, or anywhere it feels like.
      APPLIANCE

Cordially,
Ivana Pettsoon
Chairwoman

Art by Rick Stromoski

Look Both Ways!

The chicken isn't the only one crossing the road.
Match up these riddles with their punch lines to find out why.

_____ **1.** Why did the rabbit cross the road?

_____ **2.** Why did the farmer cross the road?

_____ **3.** Why did the gum cross the road?

_____ **4.** Why did the robot cross the road?

_____ **5.** Why did the dinosaur cross the road?

_____ **6.** Why did the lemur cross the road?

_____ **7.** Why did the cow cross the road?

_____ **8.** Why did the elephant cross the road?

_____ **9.** Why did the frog cross the road?

_____ **10.** Why did the dolphin cross the road?

A. Chickens weren't invented yet.

B. To get to the udder side

C. It was stuck to the chicken's foot.

D. Somebody toad him to.

E. To get to the other tide

F. It was the chicken's day off.

G. To bring back his chicken

H. To prove she could hip hop

I. To take care of some monkey business

J. He was programmed to.

Art by Jannie Ho

1.H 2.G 3.C 4.J 5.A
6.I 7.B 8.F 9.D 10.E

Just Sayin'

Give this girl something to say. Then find the hidden
BOOMERANG, **COAT HANGER**, **LIGHT BULB**, **MUG**, and **TAPE MEASURE**.

Art by David Coulson

Hamster Maze

Freckles is hungry! Can you help him find a route to the table? (He can pass by papers and seeds.) When you're done, write the letters along the way in the spaces below to answer the riddle.

START

Freckles

W H E

Z E

L S

I

L

M E O G

N G

FINISH

How long was the hamster's workout?

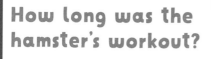

_____ _____ _____ _____ _____ _____ - _____ _____

_____ _____ _____ _____ _____

Art by Roger Simó

How long was the
hamster's workout?
WHEEL-IE LONG

Riddle Sudoku

Fill in the squares so the six letters appear only once in each row, column, and 2 x 3 box. then read the highlighted squares to find the answer to the riddle.

What do you call an undercover arachnid?

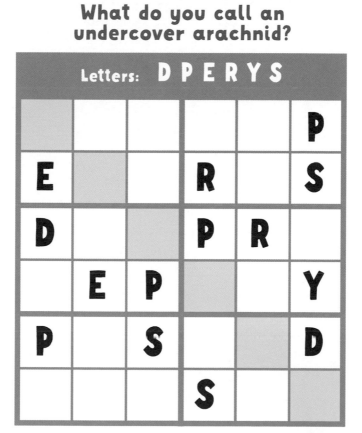

Letters: D P E R Y S

					P
E			R		S
D			P	R	
	E	P			Y
P		S			D
			S		

Answer:

A __ __ __ - __ __ __

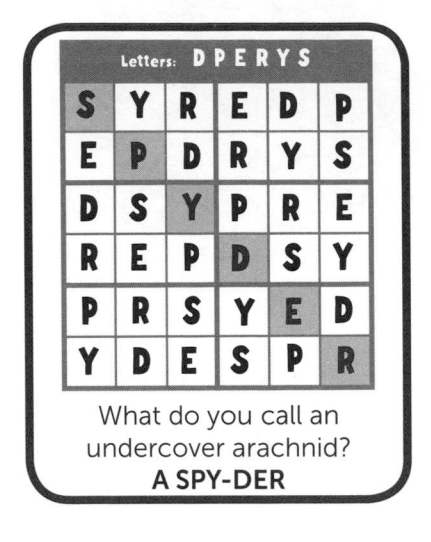

Letters: **D P E R Y S**

S	Y	R	E	D	P
E	P	D	R	Y	S
D	S	Y	P	R	E
R	E	P	D	S	Y
P	R	S	Y	E	D
Y	D	E	S	P	R

What do you call an undercover arachnid?

A SPY-DER

Letter Drop

Only six of the letters in the top line will work their way through this maze to land in the numbered spaces at the bottom. When they get there, they will spell out the answer to the riddle.

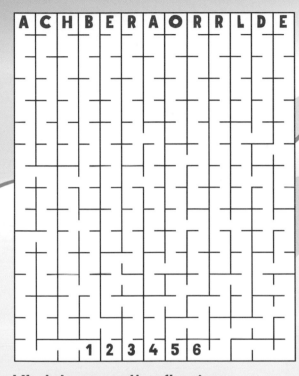

What do you call a flamingo at the North Pole?

___ ___ ___ ___ ___-___
1   2   3   4   5 6

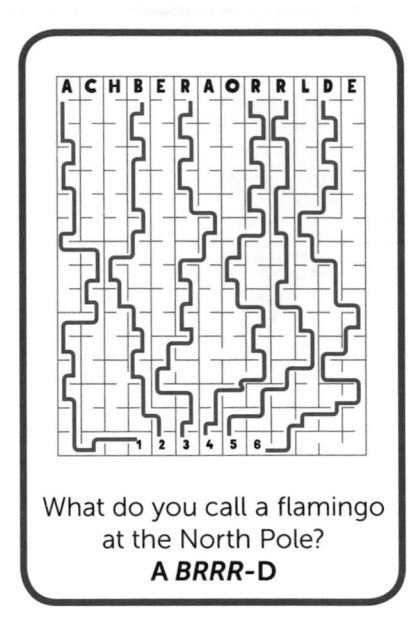

What do you call a flamingo
at the North Pole?
A *BRRR*-D

Letter Road

Drive around these roads to find the three letters that have an exact duplicate. Once you find all three letters, unscramble them to solve the riddle below.

What has cities without houses, rivers without water, and forests without trees?

A _____ _____ _____

Art by Mattia Cerato

What has cities without houses, rivers without water, and forests without trees?
A MAP

Loony Lunch

What things in this picture are silly? It's up to you!

What did one plate say to another?

"Lunch is on me!"

What do you get when you cross a potato with an elephant?

Mashed potatoes

Where do comedians go for lunch?

The laugh-eteria

Why did the clock in the cafeteria always run slow?

Every lunch it went back four seconds.

Art by Pat Lewis

Racecar Riddles

The race was won by a fraction of a second! To solve these riddles, use the fractions of the words below.

What will the school for racecars do after the summer?

First ½ of **READ**
Last ⅗ of **KAZOO**
First ¼ of **MAIL**

__ __-__ __ __ __

What did the hot dog say when it finished the race first?

Last ½ of **TRIM**
First ⅗ of **THEIR**
First ½ of **WIND**
Last ⅔ of **PEN**
Last ⅓ of **MARKER**

"__ '__ __ __ __ __ __ __ __ __!"

Where do racecars go to wash their clothes?

Last ⅗ of **BATHE**
First ½ of **LAMP**
Last ¾ of **FUND**
Last ½ of **VERY**
First ⅓ of **VET**
First ½ of **ROSE**
Last ⅗ of **BLOOM**

__ __ __ __ __ __ __ __ __ __ __

What will the school
for racecars do after
the summer?
RE-ZOOM

What did the hot
dog say when it
finished the race first?
"I'M THE WIENER!"

Where do racecars go
to wash their clothes?
THE LAUNDRY *VROOOM*

Our Annual _____ Letter
NOUN

This is best played with a friend or family member. Without letting them read the story, ask for the words or phrases under the blanks. (For example, the first thing you'll ask for is a noun.) When all the blanks are filled in, read the story out loud.

Hello, friends and family!

Well, another year has gone by. It's been quite a(n) _____ for all of us.
NOUN

Our son, _____, invented a time machine and went _____ years
TWO INITIALS — **HIGH NUMBER**

into the future. He came back with a robot named _____-_____.
NONSENSE WORD — **NUMBER**

He's very polite, even though he eats the batteries in the TV remote. Our youngest,

our darling little _____, graduated from kindergarten and will
GIRL'S NICKNAME

attend _____ in the fall. Our eldest, _____, and her famous
COLLEGE NAME — **ANOTHER GIRL'S NAME**

_____ got their own reality show!
HOUSEHOLD APPLIANCE

For our summer vacation, we went to _____, but unfortunately Dad lost
FAMOUS PLACE

all his _____ and we had to go back home. Speaking of Dad,
ARTICLE OF CLOTHING (PLURAL)

he finally broke down and got the kids a pet _____! On its first day in the
JUNGLE ANIMAL

house, it ate three _____ and 8,000 bowls of _____.
PIECE OF FURNITURE (PLURAL) — **FOOD YOU DON'T LIKE**

That about wraps it up. Happy _____, from our _____ to yours!
PLURAL NOUN — **NOUN**

Art by David Coulson

Dream Team

Each kickball jersey has a player's last name printed on it.
Can you use the clues to figure out each player's full name?

Justin is never late for practice.

Justin Thyme
_____

Jean makes super-smart plays on the field.

_____

Brock eats green vegetables to fuel up.

_____

Clara plays a woodwind instrument to relax before games.

_____

Joe loves making his teammates laugh.

_____

Crystal is good at predicting who will win.

_____

Mary never tires on the field.

_____

Kara brings after-game treats for the team.

_____

Al likes to volunteer to help the coach.

_____

Justin Thyme
Jean Yuss
Brock Lee
Clara Nett
Joe King
Crystal Ball
Mary Thon
Kara Mell
Al Dewitt

Just Sayin'

Give this boy something to say. Then find the hidden **ARROW**, **BALLOON**, **BOOK**, **GLOVE**, and **PEN**.

Art by David Coulson

Mail Call!

Can you help the postal carrier find the path to the mailbox? When you're done, write the letters along the way in the spaces below to answer the riddle.

What word has the most letters in it?

_ _ _ _ _ _ _

START

FINISH

Art by Jim Paillot

MAILBOX

What word has the
most letters in it?

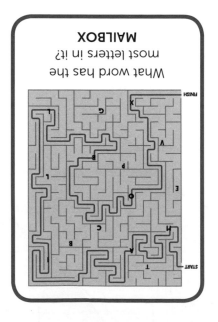

Elephant Crossing

To get the answer to the riddle below, first cross out all the pairs of matching letters. Then write the remaining letters in order in the spaces below the riddle.

QQ	BE	EE	NN	MM	OO	WW
LL	CA	SS	VV	YY	US	ZZ
ET	AA	RR	NN	HE	EE	YY
HH	XX	YL	DD	PP	UU	OV
GG	OO	ET	SS	CC	QQ	II
CC	RA	EE	MM	AA	TT	VE
LI	BB	KK	VV	ZZ	NG	TT

Why do elephants have trunks?

_ _ _ _ _ _ _   _ _ _ _

_ _ _ _   _ _ _ _ _ _ _ _ _

Art by Brian White

Tackle Box Drop

To read the joke and punch line, move the letters from each column into the boxes directly above them to form words. But watch out: the letters do not always go in the boxes in the same order as they appear. Each letter is only used once.

H	O	W		D			Y			
		O			U			C		
			H			F				?
								N		.

	T					F	C	U		
	Y	H		O		Y	I	S		
C	O	T	D	A		L	O	P	H	
W	I	M	M	U	N	I	I	N	T	
H	O	I	O	U	A	D	R	O	A	E	E

HOW DO YOU
COMMUNICATE WITH
A FISH?
YOU DROP IT A LINE.

The Key to It All

For each word hidden in the grid below, the word KEY has been replaced with 🔑. Look up, down, across, backwards, and diagonally. For the riddle answer, put the uncircled letters that are not Xs in order on the blanks.

```
X 🔑 T J S K E L E T O N 🔑 X G
M C X X O H E X O F F 🔑 X N X
A A N 🔑 T 🔑 S S A P F X I L X
L L O W U O       X X R X R X
A X M O R N       🔑 H O L E
R L R N       D O N A 🔑 X
🔑 P A D 🔑     C A R H D
I U S X H       N X M H R
X N E D C D     O P A O A
L C E T X       X T X S C O
O H C A A       X E X T 🔑 B
C X O W L       X X E X 🔑
K A S A X       K 🔑 R U T
E E R H         J 🔑 X X X
R X X 🔑 🔑 N O M R 🔑 S T O N E
🔑 S T R O K E 🔑 E S U O H C X
Y X O 🔑 D O S 🔑 H O 🔑 P O 🔑
```

Word List

- CAR KEY
- DONKEY
- HAWKEYED
- HOCKEY
- HOKEY POKEY
- HOUSE KEY
- JOCKEY
- JOKEY
- KEYBOARD
- KEY CARD
- KEYHOLE
- KEYNOTE
- KEYPAD
- KEYPUNCH
- KEYRING
- KEYSTONE
- KEYSTROKE
- KEYWORD
- LACKEY
- LATCHKEY
- LOCKER KEY
- MALARKEY
- MASTER KEY
- MONKEY
- OFF-KEY
- OKEYDOKEY
- PASSKEY
- POKEY
- REKEY
- SKELETON KEY
- SOCKEYE SALMON
- TURKEY
- TURNKEY

Where do locksmiths go on vacation?

__ __ __ __ __ __ __ __ __ __ __ __ __ __ __ __

Where do locksmiths
go on vacation?

THE FLORIDA KEYS

Wacky Winter

What things in this picture are silly? It's up to you!

What do dinosaurs wear when it's cold outside?

Jurassic Parkas

What's another name for a backwards somersault?

A wintersault

Knock, knock.
Who's there?
Snow.
Snow who?
Snow skating today. The ice is too thin!

Why can't you tell a joke while ice skating?

The ice might crack up.

Truck Tunes

Use the number pairs to solve this riddle. Move to the right to the first number and then up to the second number. Write the letters you find in the correct spaces.

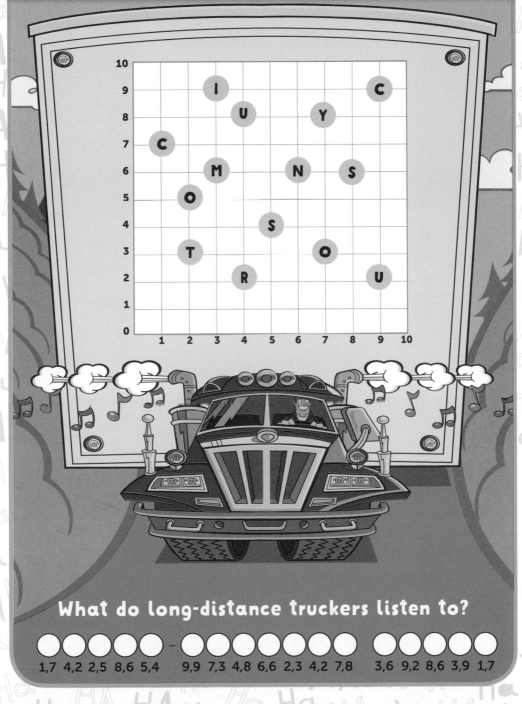

What do long-distance truckers listen to?

○○○○○ – ○○○○○○○ ○○○○○

1,7 4,2 2,5 8,6 5,4   9,9 7,3 4,8 6,6 2,3 4,2 7,8   3,6 9,2 8,6 3,9 1,7

Art by Garry Colby

What do long-distance
truckers listen to?
**CROSS-COUNTRY
MUSIC**

Please Excuse _____
YOUR FIRST NAME

This is best played with a friend or family member. Without letting them read the story, ask for the words or phrases under the blanks. (For example, the first thing you'll ask for is your first name.) When all the blanks are filled in, read the story out loud.

Please excuse _____ from school tomorrow. As you may know, our
YOUR FIRST NAME

_____ family was recently contacted by NASA and asked to
ADJECTIVE

participate in a space/time experiment. So _____ will be traveling
YOUR FIRST NAME

_____ years into the future tomorrow and will probably end
VERY HIGH NUMBER

up on the planet _____-20 in the Alpha-_____
NAME OF TOWN CLOSE BY KIND OF CAR

solar system in the _____ galaxy. By the way, all the teachers
FONT NAME

there happen to be _____ with five _____ and 20
ANIMAL (PLURAL) BODY PART (PLURAL)

_____! You would so fit in!
ANOTHER BODY PART (PLURAL)

It will certainly be a(n) _____ experience for my child, and I hope
ADJECTIVE

you agree. The plan is for _____ to bring some _____ back
YOUR FIRST NAME PLURAL NOUN

from the trip for_____-and-Tell at school. If all goes _____,
VERB -LY WORD

_____ should be back in school by _____ and
YOUR FIRST NAME YEAR IN THE FUTURE

_____ with other students!
-ING VERB

Parent of

_____
YOUR FIRST NAME

Art by Rick Stromoski

Lizard Laughs

Each lizard has one that matches it exactly.
Pair up the lizards to match each riddle with its punch line.

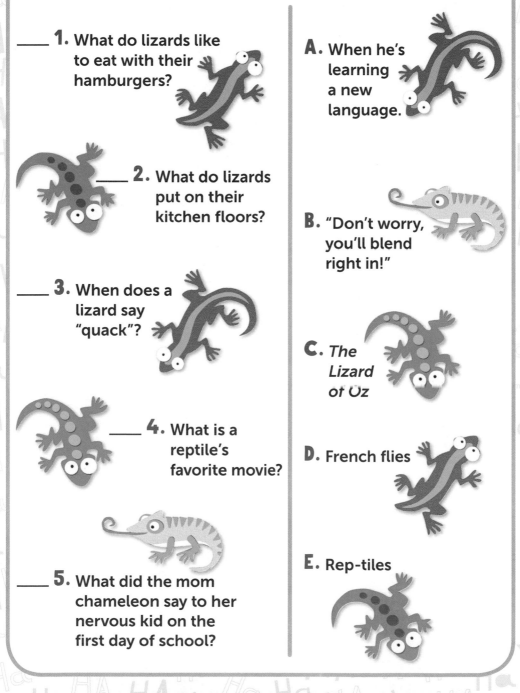

_____ **1.** What do lizards like to eat with their hamburgers?

A. When he's learning a new language.

_____ **2.** What do lizards put on their kitchen floors?

B. "Don't worry, you'll blend right in!"

_____ **3.** When does a lizard say "quack"?

C. _The Lizard of Oz_

_____ **4.** What is a reptile's favorite movie?

D. French flies

_____ **5.** What did the mom chameleon say to her nervous kid on the first day of school?

E. Rep-tiles

Just Sayin'

Give this bird something to think. Then find the hidden
BASKETBALL, **CRESCENT MOON**, **ENVELOPE**, **GLOVE**, and **TEACUP**.

Art by David Coulson

Sock Drop

It's laundry day! Can you find the correct route for this dirty sock to make it down the laundry chute? When you're done, write the letters along the way in the spaces below to answer the riddle.

Did you hear the joke about the gym sock?

—— — —————— .

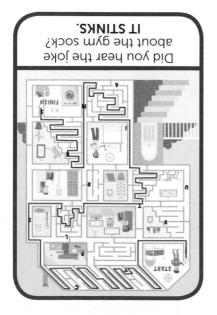

Did you hear the joke
about the gym sock?
IT STINKS.

Frog on the Go

Give a wave to these froggy friends and then use the
clues to find the five letters that answer the riddle below.

The first letter is in **sheep**, but not in **sleepy**.
The second letter is in **owl**, but not in **wild**.
The third letter is in **pig**, **wasp**, and **puppy**.
The fourth letter is in **fish**, but not in **shelf**.
The fifth letter is in **hen**, **panda**, and **lion**.

What do you say to a frog who needs a ride?

"__ __ __   __ __!"

Art by Joey Ellis

What do you say to a
frog who needs a ride?
"HOP IN!"

Market Box Drop

To read the joke and punch line, move the letters from each column into the boxes directly above them to form words. But watch out: the letters do not always go in the boxes in the same order as they appear. Each letter is only used once.

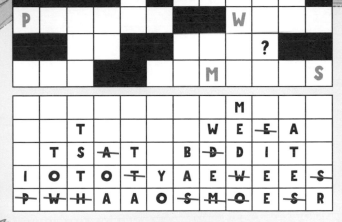

	W	H	A	T			D	O	E	S
						S				
P							W			
								?		
							M			S

								M		
	T					W	E	~~E~~	A	
	T	S	~~A~~	T		B	~~D~~	D	I	T
I	O	T	O	~~T~~	Y	A	E	~~W~~	E	E	~~S~~
~~P~~	~~W~~	H	A	A	O	S	~~M~~	~~O~~	E	~~S~~	R

Art by Josh Cleland

What's the Buzz?

There are 17 insect names hidden in this grid. Look up, down, across, and diagonally. Put the uncircled letters in order on the blanks below to see the answer to the riddle.

Word List

BEETLE
BUTTERFLY
CICADA
DRAGONFLY
EARWIG
FIREFLY
FLEA
GNAT
GRASSHOPPER
HONEYBEE
KATYDID
LADYBUG
MANTIS
MOSQUITO
STINKBUG
TERMITE
WEEVIL

```
M E R B E F C A W H
A T E T U I S E E O
N I P A T R H E E N
T M P N M E S P V E
I R O G O F G Y I Y
S E H U S L I L L B
C T S B Q Y W F A E
I I S K U A R N D E
C D A N I E A O Y T
A E R I T L E G B L
D R G T O F S A U E
A P U S I E D R G H
E B R K A T Y D I D
```

Why did the fly fly?

__ __ __ __ __ __ __ __ __ __

__ __ __ __ __ __ __ __ __ __

__ __ __ __

Why did the fly fly?
**BECAUSE THE SPIDER
SPIED HER**

Museum Mayhem

What things in this picture are silly? It's up to you!

Why do museums have old dinosaur bones?

They can't afford new ones.

Knock, knock.
Who's there?
Mozart.
Mozart who?
Mozart is found in museums.

Where does a donkey go on a field trip?

To a mule-seum

How do you know there's a woolly mammoth in your fridge?

You can't close the door.

Art by Dave Whamond

Funny Fractions

You HALF to laugh at these funny jokes!
To solve each riddle, use the fractions of the words below.

What do you call three feet of trash?

_ _ _ _ _ _ _

First ½ of **AT**
First ½ of **JUNGLE**
Last ½ of **ICKY**
Last ¾ of **CARD**

Who invented fractions?

_ _ _ _ _ _ _

_ _ _ _ _ _

Last ¾ of **WHEN**
First ⅔ of **RYE**
First ½ of **THEMES**
Last ⅔ of **SLEIGH**
Middle ⅓ of **MOTHER**

Art by Mike Moran

What do you call
three feet of trash?
A JUNKYARD

Who invented fractions?
HENRY THE EIGHTH

The Haunted _____
NOUN

This is best played with a friend or family member. Without letting them read the story, ask for the words or phrases under the blanks. (For example, the first thing you'll ask for is an adjective.) When all the blanks are filled in, read the story out loud.

One day close to Halloween, Ethan and Emily decided to look for ghosts. They put

on their Ghost Goggles, which made the real world look dark and _____.
ADJECTIVE

They stepped out of their house on Crooked _____ Lane and walked
VEGETABLE

around until they found a spooky house. Ethan knocked on the _____
COLOR

door, and it opened by itself. Then Emily saw a small _____ run
LARGE ANIMAL

under an old _____! The kids tiptoed across the creaky floor and saw
NOUN

spiderwebs the size of a(n) _____. Suddenly, the wind blew a pile of
KITCHEN APPLIANCE

dirty _____ right past their _____. Then a voice
ITEM OF CLOTHING (PLURAL)   BODY PART (PLURAL)

cried out, "Ethan? Help!" Both kids got goosebumps the size of _____.
PLANET

"Emily? Help!" the voice said. It was coming from behind a door! The kids tore off

their goggles and slowly opened the door. There stood their father, his face as

_____ as old _____, struggling with the vacuum cleaner. "Help
COLOR   LUNCHEON MEAT

me clean this messy house, and do your chores," he said. Then the kids realized that

they were back on Crooked _____ Lane . . . and in their own house!
SAME VEGETABLE

Art by David Coulson

Match Batch

It's rhyme time! Can you match each clue to the pair of rhyming words that describes it?

1. Rubber reptile

2. Squished baseball cap

3. Rabbit comedian

4. Intelligent insects

5. Happy canine

6. 16-year-old who showered

7. Brave primate

8. Sunburned noggin

9. Stinky sandwich shop

10. Child who lives on a fancy boat

A. Spunky monkey

B. Smelly deli

C. Clean teen

D. Fake snake

E. Red head

F. Yacht tot

G. Wise flies

H. Jolly collie

I. Flat hat

J. Funny bunny

Art by Jack Desrocher

1.D 2.I 3.J 4.G 5.H
6.C 7.A 8.E 9.B 10.F

Just Sayin'

Give this boy something to say. Then find the hidden
BANANA, **DOUGHNUT**, **PAPER CLIP**, **RULER**, and **TEACUP**.

Art by David Coulson

Reading Space

Time to relax for this astronaut! Follow each line from a letter to a blank space and write the letter in that space. When you are finished, you will have the answer to the riddle below.

What do astronauts like to read?

M O K O C S B T O E

Art by Mike Moran

Kiddie Ride

To figure out this riddle, follow the directions below. Each sentence will tell you where one letter is in the grid. Once you've found it, write it in the correct space below the riddle.

1. This letter is the first vowel in the top row.

2. This letter is two below the **J**.

3. Find the letter between a **Q** and a **U**.

4. This is the next-to-last letter in the bottom row.

5. This letter appears three times in the fifth row.

6. Find the letter that is directly above the **W**.

7. This letter is three above an **S**.

8. This letter is in two of the four corners.

C	V	B	O	E	S
B	A	M	R	Y	Z
R	J	N	I	X	C
E	P	Q	E	U	W
O	T	L	O	L	L
S	H	G	Y	A	R

What do babies ride at amusement parks?

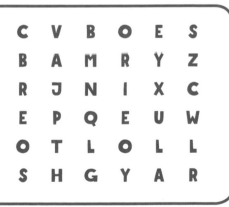

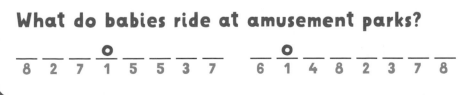

__ __ __ __O__ __ __ __ __   __ __O__ __ __ __ __ __ __
 8 2 7 1 5 5 3 7   6 1 4 8 2 3 7 8

Art by Kelly Kennedy

What do babies ride at
amusement parks?
STROLLER COASTERS

Bunny Drop

Only six of the letters in the top line will work their way through this maze to land in the numbered spaces at the bottom. When they get there, they will spell out the answer to the riddle.

R H A I P R O H C O K O P

1 2 3 4 5 6

What is a rabbit's favorite kind of music?

__ __ __-__ __ __

Art by Tamara Petrosino

What is a rabbit's
favorite kind of music?

HIP-HOP

Duck, Duck, Rhyme

Each clue below leads to an answer that rhymes with the word *duck*. Get quacking on filling them in! Then put the numbered letters in the correct spaces below to solve the riddle.

1. A four-leaf clover is considered good ___ ___ ___ ___
                                              3

2. Hit this in a hockey game. ___ ___ ___ ___
                                              5

3. Slang for a dollar ___ ___ ___ ___

4. A chicken's sound ___ ___ ___ ___ ___
                          4

5. Nickname for Charles ___ ___ ___ ___ ___

6. Pickup or eighteen-wheeler ___ ___ ___ ___ ___
                                    2

7. Nickname of Mark Twain's character Finn ___ ___ ___ ___

8. Peel the leaves and silk from an ear of corn. ___ ___ ___ ___ ___
                                                       1

9. To pull at harp strings ___ ___ ___ ___ ___

What do you call an elephant in a phone booth?

___ ___ ___ ___ ___
 1   2   3   4   5

1. LUCK
2. PUCK
3. BUCK
4. CLUCK
5. CHUCK
6. TRUCK
7. HUCK
8. SHUCK
9. PLUCK

What do you call an elephant
in a phone booth?
STUCK

Super Suds

What things in this picture are silly? It's up to you!

Why did the pig clean his car?

The farmer said, "Hogwash!"

What does a car become when it goes into the carwash?

Wet

Why did the robber go to the carwash?

He wanted to make a clean getaway.

What kind of snake keeps its car the cleanest?

A windshield viper

Art by Dave Whamond

All Aboard!

To solve each riddle, start at the arrow. Write every other letter in order in the spaces below, crossing out each letter once it's been used. Keep going until you've been to each letter exactly once.

START

How are a train and an orchestra alike?

C E O A N C D H U C A T S O A R

_ _ _ _ _

_ _ _   _

_ _ _ _ _ _ _ _ _ _ .

START

How do train engines learn to play sports?

O E A Y C H H A E V S E T C H

_ _ _ _

_ _ _ _

_ _ _ _ _ _ _ _ .

How are a train and an orchestra alike? **EACH HAS A CONDUCTOR.**

How do train engines learn to play sports? **THEY HAVE COACHES.**

My Family _____
NOUN

This is best played with a friend or family member. Without letting them read the story, ask for the words or phrases under the blanks. (For example, the first thing you'll ask for is a friend's first name.) When all the blanks are filled in, read the story out loud.

Dear _____,
FRIEND'S FIRST NAME

We just had the best family vacation! Everyone came along except

_____, whom we had to put in a kennel. First, we
SIBLING'S/ COUSIN'S NAME

went all the way to _____ to visit the Museum of the
NEARBY STREET

American _____. It was _____! Did you know that
BODY PART   ADJECTIVE

humans used to have three _____? Then we went to
SAME BODY PART
(PLURAL)

_____ World. We had to wait _____ hours in
FRIEND'S LAST NAME   HIGH NUMBER

line to get on the "Rocket to _____ City" ride, but it was so
APPLIANCE

worth it! I hurt my left _____ on the way down the last drop,
NOUN

but was okay after Mom rubbed _____ on it. Then I got the
FOOD YOU DON'T LIKE

chance to _____ a giant _____! That was awesome,
VERB   TYPE OF INSECT

but its breath smelled like deep-fried, _____-year-old
LARGE NUMBER

_____. And that was just Monday! I'll write again soon to tell
NOUN (PLURAL)

you about the rest of the trip. Bye!

Art by Rich Powell

Vacation Destinations

Each suitcase has one that matches it exactly.
Pair up the suitcases to match each traveler with its destination.

_____ **1.** Where does bacteria go on vacation?

A. Lace Vegas

_____ **2.** Where do termites go on vacation?

B. Key West

_____ **3.** Where do cows go on vacation?

C. Pennsylvania

_____ **4.** Where do sneakers go on vacation?

D. Hollywood

_____ **5.** Where do ants go on vacation?

E. The *Boohamas*

_____ **6.** Where do cars go on vacation?

F. *Moo* York

_____ **7.** Where do ghosts go on vacation?

G. Germany

_____ **8.** Where do pencils go on vacation?

H. Frants

Art by Mike Dammer

1.G **2**.D **3**.F **4**.A
5.H **6** B **7**.E **8**.C

Just Sayin'

Give this boy something to think. Then find the hidden
CANE, **FOOTBALL**, **PENCIL**, **SLICE OF PIZZA**, and **STAMP**.

Art by David Coulson

Great Skate

Suki is heading to the skate park. Can you help her find the right way to roll? When you're done, write the letters along the way in the spaces below to answer the riddle.

What's the hardest thing about learning to skateboard?

The _ _ _ _ _ _ _

START

FINISH

Art by Mike Moran

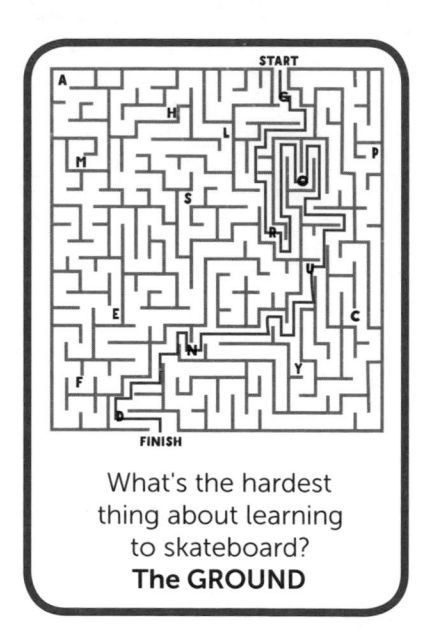

What's the hardest
thing about learning
to skateboard?
The GROUND

If at First . . .

The answer to the riddle below is easy—if you know your measurements. Each "If" statement below will give you a letter and tell you where to put it.

A. If a cup is larger than a pint, the third letter is a **U**. If not, it is an **O**.

B. If there are 100 centimeters in a meter, the first and tenth letters are **A**. If not, they are **I**.

C. If a liter is smaller than a gallon, the last letter is an **R**. If not, it is a **T**.

D. If there are three teaspoons in a tablespoon, the sixth letter is an **L**. if not, it is a **D**.

E. If there are 5,000 pounds in a ton, the seventh, ninth, and twelfth letters are **C**. If not, they are **E**.

F. If there are 1,000 grams in a kilogram, the fourth letter is a **U**. If not, it is a **V**.

G. If there are seven feet in two yards, the eighth letter is an **A**. If not, it is an **H**.

H. If a mile is longer than a kilometer, the fifth letter is a **B**. If not, it is a **T**.

I. If 1,000 millimeters equals 1 centimeter, the second and eleventh letters are **B**. If not, they are **D**.

What do you get when you cross a monster and a baseball game?

$\overline{}$ $\overline{}$ $\overline{}$ $\overline{}$ $\overline{}$ $\overline{}$ $\overline{}$ $\overline{}$ $\overline{}$ $\overline{}$ $\overline{}$ $\overline{}$ $\overline{}$
1   2 3 4 5 6 7 8 9 10 11 12 13

What do you get when you cross a monster and a baseball game?
A DOUBLEHEADER

Truck Talk Drop

To read the joke and punch line, move the letters from each column into the boxes directly above them to form words. But watch out: the letters do not always go in the boxes in the same order as they appear. Each letter is only used once.

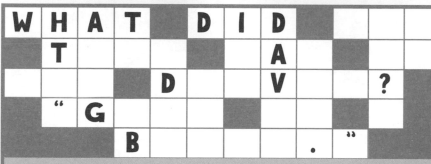

Top grid:
W	H	A	T		D	I	D			
	T						A			
				D			V			?
	"	G								
		B					.	"		

Bottom grid (letters to move):
					X					
	A	B	D	E	S	M				
H	I	R	E	A	K	D	E		A	
T	H	E	T	R	D	E	Y	R	T	E
W	T	G	I	V	R	I	A	E	T	H	O

Art by Garry Colby

WHAT DID THE TIRE
SAY TO THE DRIVER?
"GIVE ME A BRAKE."

Getting Around

There are 18 types of transportation hidden in the grid below. Look up, down, across, and diagonally. Put the uncircled letters in order on the blanks below to see the answer to the riddle.

Word List
BIKE
CANOE
CAR
KAYAK
MOTORCYCLE
PLANE
ROWBOAT
SAILBOAT
SCOOTER
SHIP
SUBWAY
TAXI
TRACTOR
TRAIN
TRUCK
TUGBOAT
VAN
WAGON

```
T U G B O A T R H M
E A R B K U R E O S
S A O C I O S T N H
C U U B T K O O I I
I R B C W R E O A P
T X A W C O E C R S
H R A Y A K R S T C
T I C T A Y V A N A
S L R Y E N A L P N
E T A O B L I A S O
O K W A G O N A R E
```

How does a lion paddle his canoe?

_ _ _   _ _ _   _ _ _ _ _ _ _

Art by Jack Desrocher

How does a lion paddle
his canoe?
HE USES HIS ROAR.

Amusing Market

What things in this picture are silly? It's up to you!

Why do bees have sticky hair?

Because they use honeycombs

Knock, knock.
Who's there?
Farmer.
Farmer who?
Farmer people here than there were last week.

What kind of nut always seems to have a cold?

Cashew!

What do penguins wear on their heads?

Ice caps

Art by Gary LaCoste

Compass Comedy

Start at the North (N) circle. Then move in the directions listed below. As you move to each new circle, write the letter you find there in the correct space to answer the riddle.

Why was the broom running late?

1. S 1 ___
2. SW 2 ___
3. SE 1 ___
4. E 3 ___
5. NW 2 ___
6. E 1 ___
7. N 1 ___
8. W 3 ___
9. S 4 ___
10. E 2 ___
11. NE 2 ___ .

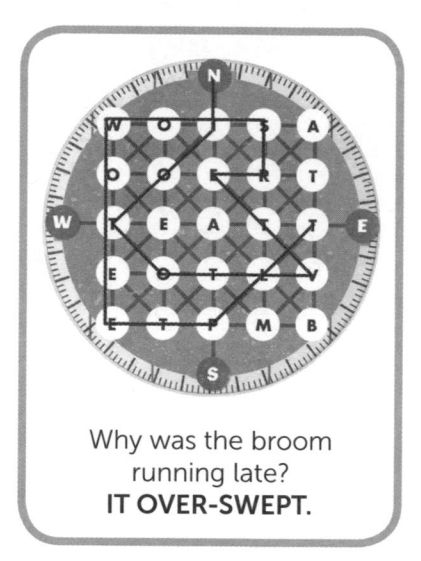

Why was the broom
running late?
IT OVER-SWEPT.

A Brand-New _____
NOUN

This is best played with a friend or family member. Without letting them read the story, ask for the words or phrases under the blanks. (For example, the first thing you'll ask for is your first name.) When all the blanks are filled in, read the story out loud.

Hi, friends. I'm here to tell you about a great new product: _____'s
YOUR FIRST NAME

Miracle _____! Now watch this: I'm going to rub a school backpack
NOUN

with _____ along with some dried _____ and
SMELLY FOOD   FRUIT

_____ jelly sauce. Then I'll pour some _____ on
VEGETABLE   LIQUID OTHER THAN WATER

it. And look: Just _____ on it five times and . . . not only is the stain
VERB

gone, but take a peek *inside* the backpack. All the homework is now done, and

every subject is _____ percent correct!
LOW NUMBER

But that's not all! Inside this backpack's pocket is a *brand-new* _____!
NOUN

Yes, it comes *free* with your order! And did we also mention the lifetime supply of

_____?
FOOD YOU LOVE

Folks, you'd normally have to go to _____ to get this very special
DISTANT PLANET

product. But if you call now, this amazing _____ can be yours for just
NOUN

_____ million dollars! Call now!
VERY HIGH NUMBER

ALL NEW! AMAZING! COOL!

Art by David Coulson

Name Game

Can you match each of these 10 funny book titles to their author?
Try reading the author names out loud!

1. *Always Be Prepared*

2. *How to Write a Best Seller*

3. *Snakes of the Jungle*

4. *Tumbling Made Easy*

5. *How to Make a Movie*

6. *You Can Be a Weight Lifter*

7. *Wild Felines of North America*

8. *Stop and Smell the Flowers*

9. *A Math Story*

10. *My Life as a Basketball Star*

A. Rose Bush

B. Ada Lot

C. Jim Nast

D. Justin Case

E. Anna Conda

F. Duncan Score

G. Holly Wood

H. Paige Turner

I. Bea Strong

J. Bob Katz

Art by Kelly Kennedy

Just Sayin'

Give this ant something to say. Then find the hidden
BASEBALL, **CARROT**, **HEART**, **RULER**, and **SCISSORS**.

Art by James Kochalka

Go Cart!

Riley's cart is so full she can hardly see! Can you help her find the right path to the checkout counter? When you're done, write the letters along the way in the spaces below to answer the riddle.

What do you get if you put groceries in a go-kart?

___ ___ ___ ___   ___ ___ ___

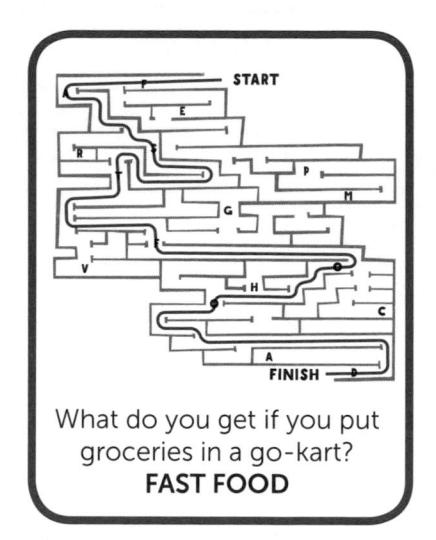

What do you get if you put groceries in a go-kart?

FAST FOOD

Riddle Sudoku

Fill in the squares so the six letters appear only once in each row, column, and 2 x 3 box. then read the highlighted squares to find the answer to the riddle.

What do you call a sick pony?

Letters: A R H E S O

	R		S		
A					
	H		E	O	
	S	O		H	
					H
	H			R	

Answer:

A little __ __ __ __ __ __ __ __

What do you call
a sick pony?
A little HOARSE

Letters: **A R H E S O**

Farm Box Drop

To read the joke and punch line, move the letters from each column into the boxes directly above them to form words. But watch out: the letters do not always go in the boxes in the same order as they appear. Each letter is only used once.

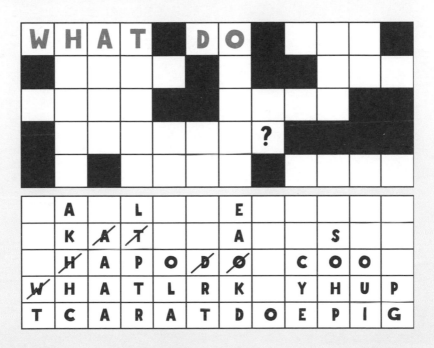

Grid:
WHAT DO ...

Letter columns:
	A		L		E			
	K	A̶	T̶		A		S	
	H̶	A	P	O	D̶	O̶	C	O	O
W̶	H	A	T	L	R	K	Y	H	U	P
T	C	A	R	A	T	D	O	E	P	I	G

Art by Julissa Mora

Scrambled States

Can you figure out which eight state names are scrambled here?
Each answer is one word. Then put the numbered letters in
the correct spaces under the riddle to reveal the answer.

1. A HUT   U   T   A   H
           2

2. TAXES   ___ ___ ___ ___ ___

3. NO OGRE   ___ ___ ___ ___ ___ ___

4. I GO RAGE   ___ ___ ___ ___ ___ ___ ___
                4

5. ANT MOAN   ___ ___ ___ ___ ___ ___ ___

6. LOOK, A HAM   ___ ___ ___ ___ ___ ___ ___ ___
                      1

7. AFRICAN OIL   ___ ___ ___ ___ ___ ___ ___ ___ ___ ___
                  3

8. TEEN SENSE   ___ ___ ___ ___ ___ ___ ___ ___ ___

What state is round at each end and high in the middle?

___ ___ ___ ___
 1   2   3   4

Art by Jim Paillot

1. UTAH
2. TEXAS
3. OREGON
4. GEORGIA
5. MONTANA
6. OKLAHOMA
7. CALIFORNIA
8. TENNESSEE

What state is round at each end and high in the middle?

OHIO

Topsy-Turvy Toys

What things in this picture are silly? It's up to you!

Why did the snake go to the toy store?

To get a new rattle

What's a ghost's favorite toy?

A boo-merang

Why doesn't a teddy bear wear socks?

He prefers to go barefoot.

Knock, knock.

Who's there?

Castle.

Castle who?

You castle lot of questions, don't you?

Art by Dave Whamond

Three's a Crowd

10	12	16	33	8	22	24	11	25	13	40
P	T	A	H	A	S	E	G	A	T	D
15	42	20	30	60	16	18	7	44	36	54
B	E	L	R	M	C	U	H	S	D	A
4	21	48	14	57	39	35	51	45	63	27
D	T	R	Q	I	A	S	N	G	L	E

Where did the Three Musketeers go on vacation?

___ ___ ___   ___ ___ ___ ___ ___ ___ ___   ___ ___ ___ ___ ___ ___ ___ ___

Art by Steve Skelton

Where did the
Three Musketeers
go on vacation?
THE BERMUDA TRIANGLE

A Letter from _____
PLACE

This is best played with a friend or family member. Without letting them read the story, ask for the words or phrases under the blanks. (For example, the first thing you'll ask for is a body part.) When all the blanks are filled in, read the story out loud.

Dear Family,

Today is my second day at Camp Fractured _____. What a busy day!
BODY PART

I went on a nature walk and got _____ mosquito bites. I rubbed some
BIG NUMBER

_____ on them, but it didn't help. In the afternoon soccer game, I scored
YUCKY FOOD

_____ goals, but that's because there was no goalie. Then, I kayaked
REALLY BIG NUMBER

down the Great Three-Pronged _____-quihanna River, but halfway
FRUIT

down the rapids, I realized there was no kayak. Later, I tried to make a lanyard out

of _____, but it didn't come out too well. Maybe I'll try to make a(n)
SOMETHING GROSS

_____ out of _____ instead.
NOUN   PLURAL NOUN

I'm in Wild _____ Cabin, but I'm the only kid in here. Actually, there's
SMALL ANIMAL

only one cabin at this camp. Also, there are no counselors or _____.
PLURAL NOUN

I'm really just in our backyard, so please open the door and let me in because my

_____ is getting cold!
BODY PART

Art by Kevin Rechin

Laugh Out Loud

LOL usually stands for Laugh Out Loud.
Can you use the clues to identify the rest of these LOLs?

1. Jump in Autumn

2. Slow woodwind bedtime song

3. Pretty apes go to school

4. Crustaceans with a reputation

5. Wash large ballet outfits

6. Big cats giggle strangely

7. Enjoy stinky cheese

A. Launder Oversize Leotards

B. Lovely Orangutans Learn

C. Leap Onto Leaves

D. Leopards Oddly Laugh

E. Lazy Oboe Lullaby

F. Love Odorous Limberger

G. Legendary Old Lobsters

Just Sayin'

Give this girl something to say. Then find the hidden
BROCCOLI, **ENVELOPE**, **FEATHER**, **HAMMER**, and **LOLLIPOP**.

Art by James Kochalka

Flip for It

Chase just flipped his flying disc to his dog, Otto. Can you find the path the disc will take to reach Otto? When you're done, write the letters along the way in the spaces below to answer the riddle.

What kind of dog chases anything that's red?

__ __ __ __ __ __ __

Art by Mike Moran

What kind of dog chases
anything that's red?

A BULLDOG

START

FINISH

Boating Blunders

To figure out this riddle, follow the directions below. Each sentence will tell you where one letter is in the grid. Once you've found it, write it in the correct space below the riddle.

1. This letter is three down from the **X**.

2. This letter is the only vowel in the second row.

3. This letter is two up from the **Q**.

4. This letter is sandwiched between two **E**s.

5. This is the second letter in the last row.

6. This letter is the first and last in its row.

7. This letter appears side by side in the same row.

8. This letter is the first letter in the grid.

9. This letter is the only consonant in its column.

R	P	A	X	A	L	Z
T	A	B	F	W	G	M
S	Z	J	F	E	W	S
K	H	O	T	O	I	D
B	N	M	R	I	G	G
Y	E	N	E	U	Q	C

What did the boy get when he leaned over the back of the boat?

___   ___   ___   ___   ___   ___   ___   ___   ___   ___   ___   ___   ___
2   6   1   5   8   4   9   2   8   4   3   4   7

What did the boy get
when he leaned over
the back of the boat?
A STERN WARNING

Shoe Drop

Only six of the letters in the top line will work their way through this maze to land in the numbered spaces at the bottom. When they get there, they will spell out the answer to the riddle.

R A T H O Z P R C S K O E

1 2 3 4 5 6

What animal always sleeps with its shoes on?

___ ___ ___ ___ ___ ___
1   2   3   4   5   6

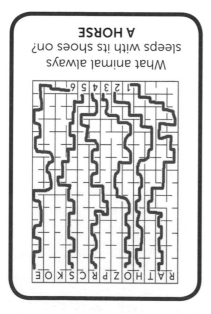

What animal always
sleeps with its shoes on?
A HORSE

Car Carriers

Use the clues below to fill in the answer spaces. Each answer starts with the letters C-A-R. Then put the numbered letters in the correct spaces under the riddle to reveal the answer.

1. Milk container   CAR__ __ __
     2

2. Orange veggie   CAR__ __ __
     1

3. Comic strip   CAR__ __ __ __

4. Feeling ill while driving   CAR__ __ __ __
     5

5. Red bird   CAR__ __ __ __ __
     3

6. A fair   CAR__ __ __ __ __
     7

7. Merry-go-round   CAR__ __ __ __ __
     4

8. Meat eater   CAR__ __ __ __ __ __

9. A woodworker   CAR__ __ __ __ __ __
     6

What would happen if all the cars in the country were painted pink?

It would be a __ __ __ __   CAR-__ __ __ __ __ __.
     6   3   2   5   2   7   1   3   4   2

1. CARTON
2. CARROT
3. CARTOON
4. CARSICK
5. CARDINAL
6. CARNIVAL
7. CAROUSEL
8. CARNIVORE
9. CARPENTER

What would happen if all the cars in the country were painted pink?
**It would be a
PINK CAR-NATION.**

Funny Field Day

What things in this picture are silly? It's up to you!

FIELD DAY

COACH

CHIPS

Knock, knock.
Who's there?
Tire.
Tire who?
Tire shoe before you trip!

Why did the baseball player leave in the middle of the game?
His coach told him to run home.

What do you get when you cross a kangaroo with a snake?
A jump rope

What do you call a Hawaiian celebration?
A hula-day

Art by Joey Ellis

Punny Kitchen

There's lots of laughter in the kitchen today!
To solve these riddles, use the fractions of words given below.

What is a math teacher's favorite dessert?

_ _ _ _ _ _ _ _ _

First ⅓ of **PIG**
First ½ of **UMPIRE**
First ¾ of **KING**
First ⅓ of **PILLOW**

Which knight helped King Arthur build his round table?

_ _ _ _ _ _ _ _ _ _ _

First ⅔ of **SIT**
Last ⅔ of **ARC**
Last ½ of **PLUM**
First ½ of **FERRET**
First ½ of **SENTENCE**

Art by Mike Moran

What is a
math teacher's
favorite dessert?
PUMPKIN PI

Which knight helped
King Arthur build
his round table?
SIR CIRCUMFERENCE

A Thank-You _____
NOUN

This is best played with a friend or family member. Without letting them read the story, ask for the words or phrases under the blanks. (For example, the first thing you'll ask for is a friend's first name.) When all the blanks are filled in, read the story out loud.

Dear _____ ,
FRIEND'S FIRST NAME

Thanks for my birthday present, the brand-new Ultra-_____
NOUN

-o-Matic Micro Plus! I've wanted one of those for _____ days! I
SMALL NUMBER

just went out and bought the _____ AA batteries it needs and
LARGE NUMBER

turned it on. Wow! It purrs just like a(n) _____ _____
ADJECTIVE   COLOR

_____ when it's on " _____ mode." It exploded once
WILD ANIMAL   ADJECTIVE

and destroyed our _____ , but otherwise it's
PIECE OF LIVING ROOM FURNITURE

operating smoothly.

I plugged our _____ into it. In just a few seconds, out came five
APPLIANCE

pounds of _____ ! I was so happy! I had no idea that this new
SNACK FOOD

_____ was so different from the _____ -o-Matic
NOUN   NOUN

Micro!

I can't wait until your birthday, when I can get you something just as

_____ !
ADJECTIVE

Thanks again,

_____
YOUR FIRST NAME

Art by Peter Grosshauser

Under Umbrellas

Each umbrella has one that matches it exactly.
Pair up the umbrellas to match each riddle with its punch line.

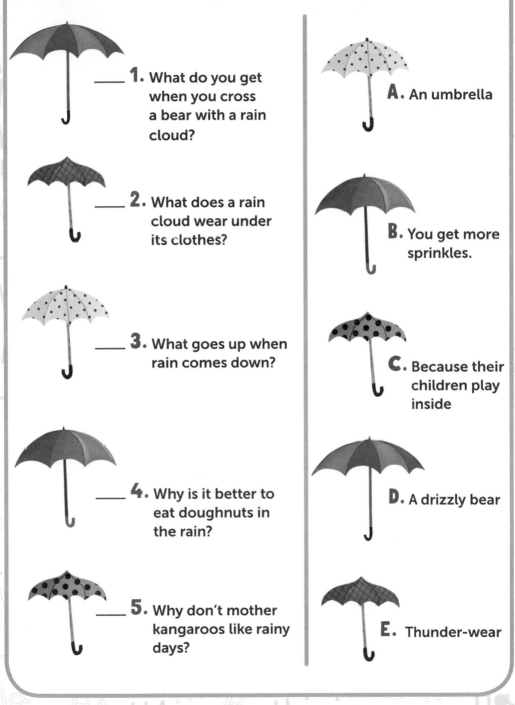

_____ **1.** What do you get when you cross a bear with a rain cloud?

A. An umbrella

_____ **2.** What does a rain cloud wear under its clothes?

B. You get more sprinkles.

_____ **3.** What goes up when rain comes down?

C. Because their children play inside

_____ **4.** Why is it better to eat doughnuts in the rain?

D. A drizzly bear

_____ **5.** Why don't mother kangaroos like rainy days?

E. Thunder-wear

1.D 2.E 3.A 4.B 5.C

Just Sayin'

Give this bird something to say. Then find the hidden
COMB, ICE-CREAM CONE, PENCIL, PLUNGER, and UMBRELLA.

Art by James Kochalka